THE MOON'S SONG

Also by Adele David:
Becoming (Migrant Press)

THE MOON'S SONG

Adele David

KATABASIS

Copyright © Adele David 2001
First published 2001 by Katabasis
10 St Martin's Close, London NW1 0HR (020 7485 3830)
katabasis@katabasis.co.uk
http://www.katabasis.co.uk

Printed and bound by Antony Rowe,
Chippenham (01249 659705)

Needlepoint pictures by Adele David:
Front cover illustration: *The Moon's Song*
Back cover illustration: *Alchemical Trees*

Typeset in-house mainly in 12 point Garamond
ISBN: 0 904872 35 1

Trade distribution: Central Books
99 Wallis Road, London E9 5LN (020 8986 4854)

KATABASIS is grateful for the support of London Arts:

LONDON ARTS

CONTENTS

ACKNOWLEDGMENTS

Acknowledgments are due to the editors of the following
publications, where some of the poems first appeared:
*Fire, Festschrift AJA, IAAP Newsletter 19, Launde Bag, Owl, Still,
The Poet's Voice and Time Haiku.*

For Ilya, Leona, Sam and Millie

The Goat Woman

Frost on the forest of the mountain.
The goat woman steps out of a cut
in the hedge. Bent, arthritic, observant
as the goats huddled behind her.
She aims guttural Tuscan at me.
I am startled, understand nothing.
Eyes sharper than before
she starts a half-hearted second round;
sees a foreign fool sitting on stone,
mid-winter, by a stony path,
pen and paper in gloved hands.
Her snowy goats, heads to one side,
make a semi-circle far enough away to feel safe.
The old woman clicks her tongue,
makes goat sounds to soothe, to move them along.
They dance off, follow their brittle leader,
feet hardly touching earth. I am left with echoes
from the valleys and villages below.
Bombarding dogs. Boys shouting. Birds. Gunshot.
A mid-morning cockerel pinches coldness closer.
Not one word from the tip of my pen.

Wall Decorations

On his white horse centre stage
Niccolo da Tolentino sits
topped by his gorgeous
gold and red patterned hat,
proper fifteenth century fashion plate,
in the middle of The Skirmish
or The Battle, a view dependent
on being Florentine or Siennese.

Uccello painted three battle scenes
for guests to gaze on during Cosimo's
banquets to show off skills in perspective,
colour, patterning. Real gold, and real silver
now tarnished to a lead grey, were used
for the horses trappings and for the men's
armour. All chivalric make-believe.

On the left side of the Battle of San
Romano is a surplus of legs,
and on the right not enough. The Medici
insignia of three feathers is repeated
on helmets, their star emblem becomes
the calyx of white roses. Signs not symbols.
As Donatello said: These things
are of no use except for marquetry.

Somebody's Got to Make the Meals

Velásquez: Christ in the House of Martha and Mary

My hands get red and chapped
from being wet. They burn
with chilli, and smell of garlic.
That's fine by me.
The others don't want to know
what l like — the grain of the table
feeling good on my fingers;
the gutted fish all smelty cream,
glittery in the bowl;
or the weight of hard boiled eggs,
how they shine, and the special roll
they make on the plate.
We're so everyday
we don't get noticed.

Duccio's Annunciation

And when she saw him, she was troubled at his saying, and cast in her mind what manner of salutation this should be.

— LUKE 1:29

I step back, submissive to the times,
hold a veil over my heart
ready to wait two thousand years

before return to Assumption.
Gabriel enters my womb
through his staff and the lilies

that were once mine.
His hand bestows benediction
onto me who is Benediction.

I am the Triple Goddess.
Am Baalat and Mariamne
whose altars Yahveh smashed.

Now I become the Gate of Heaven,
the Interceder,
three Marys at the foot of the cross.

Humility, Virginity, Obedience
conceal I am the Giver of Life,
the Great Love that is creation.

Voices From the Maestra

We, the lilies of the field
in the Song of Solomon,
appear with the angel
at the Annunciation.

Duccio's five
from his Paradise garden,
we were the flowers of Aphrodite
before Mary.

We are the Milky Way
fallen to earth
from the Queen
of Heaven's breasts.

Sacred to Astarte,
we hide in the Divine Lady's
Canaanite name —
Lilith.

Grass Flowers

How could this be the Beloved
at the Court of a Friend?

When night and a blandness
of green set in
doubt is only a way of thinking.

The tapestry being woven
is a fixed and fruitful place
unfinished till we die.

The Talmud says
every blade of grass
has its angel bending over
whispering: Grow. Grow.

You have to be quick
to be a life threaded with flowers.

Real Life

When I grew into knowing
and people travelled
from the four directions
to carry off my healing gifts
on the backs of their Water
Buffalo — then she appeared.

Aphrodite, sun-filled on the edge
of the crowd, showed me
backward somersaults
that made all her clothes fall off.
I took her for a prostitute.
She was so happy:
there was no smile on my face.

When I realised my mistake
I left everything, rushed to the city,
knocked on doors to find her.

She showed herself among a group
of look-alikes leaving a house
with swinging, louvered doors,
and glanced back to make sure
I followed in the crowds
hurrying to the market-place.

Trying to catch up I lost her.
She knew I searched,
and watched over me,
though I've rarely glimpsed her
until now.

Chosen

Imagination glides over obstacles
like revolutions of the moon
whispering at noon in the shadow garden
in the narrows between mercy and not,
between the curtain of delight and night.

Dressed in her golden eyes
girdle firmly closed at the hip
she recites the names of his gold;
dreams fall between her fingers
as petals of acacia, and fat oleander.

Summer is as solid as his thighs.
He deals the left hand
respects her cradle of knowledge
so calamity doesn't spread.
The goddess knows all the words
for re-inventing the rose.

Lovely As She Is

At noon travelling forest fast
she of the peacock girdle,
untroubled by humility,
spreads calamity with a caress.
She appears lily-clear by sweet water,
knows all the words in the right order.
This Lillith that lives next door
uncovers beds of bent roses:
she is the carnage of the year.
I paint the walls of her house with blood.

The peacock girdle is Aphrodite's girdle of beauty.

Spring

She leaves trails of narcissi —
pale hairs on bare earth
through Easter's frost and snow.
Who, now, can touch the hem
of her dress as she passes?
Who can bow down so low?

Wettest

As clay encloses rain
overflow water
forms ditches
where blackbirds bathe.

The bright lawn
becomes a marshland
that can't be cut;
dandelions and daisies thrive.

Spires of land cress,
an exuberance of white,
bounce among the spinach
and along the bare patch
edging the true pond.

Spears of convolvulus spread
as only landowners can.
Here's a spring so wet
even light becomes globules.

And here's the late apple blossom
all fired with red,
promising juice-dripping days
running far as the elbow.

What She Did

Smooth as the wet curves
of a seaside pebble
he stood before her on the dark beach.

Then came the sun like a trumpet
blaring over horned poppies and thrift.

Words rich as gravel, knee-graze
cuts told her building plans
to block out his light.

She was a tight,
umbrella-furled narcissus.

His eyes were a glaze
of sudden frost,
his face a vista of fracture.

A stranded dolphin,
he froze on the shingle, unable.

Carrying the Garden

Marigolds, white marguerites and Margot
lived on the other side of Letty's hedge.
Letty's mother said
Margot screamed in her sleep,
refuge from Hitler's war. That year
and all the years she could remember
the war continued in Letty's garden;
splinter-sharp, death-blossoming summers.

Each day Letty peered
between tall defences of privet
that bit through fingers to the bone.
Beyond the barricade was a sunlit land
where Margot smiled
as her new brother laughed
when her new father clowned
to make them happy.

In Letty s garden no flowers grew.
No one played. The fruit trees died.
There was a crazy-paving path
and grass boggy from the last rains.
Each day she walked the rounds of the path,
counting, recounting the cracks,
retracing her steps, wishing her luck to change.

Once she was asked to a party in the garden
on the other side of the hedge.
There were piles of white pebbles to jump on,
grass grew as high as her thighs,
seed heads popped a lightness
she was unaccustomed to.
The littlest there, she spoke to no one,
thought no one spoke to her.

Given a green-stoned ring she was entranced,
lost herself within the gift
that disappeared in minutes among tall grasses.
Marigolds turned on one stem
buds, flowers, seeds, their rancid smell
insistent as the failing sun. White marguerites,
Margot, faded in the greying breeze.

Lost

She tried for sharpness
in a spiked world,
drove half under a truck
to be quick like the rest.
Real drivers raised their eyes in disgust.

When she found the mountain
she took the wrong fork,
it led to the shingle path
so she stood there crying.

People came out of their houses to help
but she was long passed remembering
where she lived.

Party

1

On the ocean of pale ash floor
absent of furniture, I stand deserted
by the people who brought me.

Our host the pop star
of the soon to begin party
in this sun filtered, love-shaped room
calls from the far wall like an old friend:
I knew you'd come. I'd a premonition.
We've never met before.

The wound he cuts in my left wrist
where the rivers of the body meet
binds us. He gently watches
as I move about in the space faintly smiling,
looking up, admiring plant forms
of lace-paper mobiles in a shallow breeze.

2

In the narrow cabin
where each wall can be touched
when standing in the centre,
my eldest daughter, who's also my sister,
shows me her sleeping infant
clothed in white, shrouded in black.

Excited at holding him close
I stain the babygrow at chest and toes,
make alchemical colours; black, red, white,
as I hold the family history in my arms.

I want to take him to the cafe
with his mother. She says
since giving birth no one goes,
other mothers eat elsewhere
or have food sent to their rooms.
As the pop star owns the boat
I'll speak to him, ask for remedy.

Magician

The magician wears a raven on his head
and holds a hoop in his hand.
I know where he went to school.

Cascading mind with movement
and time not standing still as he does now
whispering into the megaphone, midwinter.

Soon he'll go into the forest
placating platypuses,
chanting over and over: Peace.

Touching the Earth was not his ancestry
until he met Dread who lives with Dearth
where fire sits at the centre

when he thought he knew everything.
But that's not where he comes from —
I remember him dating Penelope.

Ravens

There is commotion
winging in
like life spans of Gondor,
dark caverns issuing smoke.
But they are glossy.
Each feather smooth
as long, black lakes.
When they see me they scatter
to far off aspens
then circle back squarking in flight.
Dark angels over the roof
whose wingspan
covers the four corners of vision
dream-laden from single eyed Odin.
Loud mouthed Commanders
ordered to where?

Rapunzel's Prince

Rapunzel's Prince
thrown from the tower into the thicket
climbs in a blurred nimbus of memory
his separation years.
Treading in stone shoes,
desert days that like a ball of magic twine
unravel a never-ending road.

His once brief gathering
homed two nights
of armfuls of delight.
Now his back, bent like a reaper's,
knows its harvest well,
fills his wandering way,
a prince of tears.

White Cabbage

Swimming-pool-pale in sunlight, subtler than kiwi,
this roll of a weak, sweet-mint-teaball
knows no exile, knows how to thrive everywhere.

Earth's sorbet moon replicated in rows
is stacked onto lorries for market,
pyramided on barrows to be sold.

Leaf after tight packed leaf
is compact as a solid back, and as handsome.
Some layers are unpeelable without breaking.

A freezy disdain only smells under the nose.
Crispness crackles and splits to exude juice
thick as milk, mildly acidic against the teeth.

Distant cousin to a rindless lemon:
hold your breath,
white cabbage illumines a whole head of hearing.

Purple Orchids

A woman in a hem-bedraggled, purple coat
and me beside her contemplating orchids
in a Waitrose hothouse when she turns
and peers at me surreptitious, stage-whispering:

Flowers are expensive here, they last longer
from Marks what with the feed they come with.
I need these purple orchids to blossom up
a dull corner, white walls shadowed-over

with deities. Slow motion bludgeoning bursting
from a tall, narrow vase as they jump for space
pouting in varying directions, wax buds flecked
a white-green. What was exotic when I was ten

is now supermarket fare. The cheapest,
longest lasting flowers, Thailanders, sometimes
brought by a friend straight from his plane,
live more than five weeks.

Heart Chakra

Sharp into crystal
the snow on the mountain.
Do not be a fool, said the teacher,
let the past go.

I clung to the outmoded,
swung on a kitchen cupboard
so many feet above kitchens
I could not count the footsteps
towards cooking
until the cupboard door hung
right-angled towards death,
before finally letting go.

Grey as a mass of smoke
the heart, Anahata, is open,
is vermilion,
black as an antelope,
more than the heart's desire.

Sharp into crystal
the snow on the mountain.
When I met my Lord
I did not know him.

The Hours of the Day

In the blood of the cup
fire and ice cauterise me.
From burning to burning I am renamed,
reduced to powders, to liquidity.

The insoluble does not die.
I do not die.
I am the ashes of the flower,
the bird of the stone.

How could I ask of my dilemma:
throw away this stone.
It is my journey
and my foundation.

Solid Tears

South-westerly behind the kitchen sink
runs the caul canal —
earth so bitter the mouth dries.

We follow the dwarf child,
my second self and I,
tunnelling towards the Mothers;
knees, faces, hands showing their scars.

Along the earth-fall tunnel
unfamiliar shapes flicker.
Incubi. Succubi. Homunculi.

Reflected fires leap against the glass.
Grotesque faces press against the panes
eyeing us. A progression of talons,
claws, articulate mouths.

Crouching beyond the passage,
in the laboratory,
the arc lights blind me.

I cannot comprehend the command: Drink.
The phial with the silver embryo
is thrust against my mouth, cuts my mouth.
The child in the waters undulates —

is turning, turning, turning.
Drink, commands the Mother,
towering in her long, white coat:
South-westerly is obeying me.
Seeking the key to turn night into day
I swallow the embryo,
the silver tench, child.

Hermes

Into harbour they sailed
telescoped together
playing the well-brought-up,
friendship bound.

They found Hermes, the messenger,
the connecter of dreams,
master of treachery.

The sea visitors, capable of love,
but unprovided for,
practised old arts
in an alien land.

Fascinated with boundlessness
Hermes played his games,
bounced in and out of their lives.

His harsh note hung in the ear.
Sobered by his tempering music
they went navigating beyond day
into unknown frontiers.

Giver to the received,
king of no country,
Hermes laughed.

Listening to the Angel

He who was a fair hand at trickery
lay blind-eyed waiting on air,
waiting, waiting for stillness
when the angel came, came with a soft gliding
of down wings, hovering over the stone.

Jacob's hip had no comforter.
No black veiled city dweller
revealed a smile that withdrew pain,
made his body whole, returned him
happy to his people. Jacob,
maker of white ewes into brown,
could have gone back to a silence
where there was no Dachau, no ovens,
no Wotan with hands full of ash.

If there had been no fight with the angel
before Bildad knew about spiders,
before David and Jonathan,
those wandering tribes
would have had no alliance,
would have gone their ways
swallowed up by Baal or Allah.
Nothing would have remained
to fill those high chimneys
with the People of the Word.

Persona

Though we'd not talked
through twenty years
time didn't seem to conquer
old habits, the fascination
of your face in that day's paper
fresh as then: agitation
still ripe with might-have-beens.
Not ever lovers
though your wife thought so.
Then by chance we met
in my supermarket, and no,
you're no longer live —
an old man brittle with fame.

Passages

For L.G.

She gave a party for her new man
who had just moved in
whom nobody else had met.

An old flame came from Zurich
to make the cream dessert.
Another friend brought the plates.

August. Feast of the Assumption. Both
wearing white. All night guests remark
on their eyes reflecting each other.

Next morning, before the dishes
were washed, his decision was made
to move back to his wife and family.

Left behind, on his side of the bed,
with the keys, the birthday gift:
bronze, antique egg breaking-open.

Dr. Dufortu

Dr. Dufortu, doctor of philosophy,
                          sips tea under canvas,
his latest fancy travelling the Nile,
                          on the last room-fan cruiser.
he believes air-conditioning is a battery for germs.

Below a white hat, a green eye-shade
lessens the angularity of features on a bony frame.
His beaky nose narrows at the bridge,
                          always frowning;
the skin blotched and saggy with seventy years.
A white moustache over a lipless mouth
                          above a vulture neck.
The voice surprisingly melodic, yet precise.

Brilliant white shoes, shorts, shirt.
Limbs of a teenager, gangly and overlong.
Knees crossed, one foot swinging at the absurdity
                          of the couple across the table.
One hand, fingers yellowed from tobacco,
                          jerks like the tongue of a parrot.
A bachelor habitually worrying to be elsewhere,
                          habitually adjusting his watch.

Tu Fu in Tufnell Park

First quarter moon in August haze.
The widowed poet
relaxing on the slatted bench
examines the night sky.
The wooden table
holds an empty wine bottle
and a glass.
Moonlight silvers the eucalyptus.

In the small hours
in the tiny, walled garden
he rubs the side of his nose,
his nails broken and black,
and notes backroom lights
going out the whole street long.
Police sirens in the distance.

Tu Fu mumbles verse
and smoothes his frayed suit.
From a nearby backyard come two wails
as the cat-skirmish night opens out.

Eucalyptus Window

For Jules Cashford

Hour after hour
when the body hurts
she watches
favoured jays feed
in a clutter of colour
as squirrels gather acorns
from the bedroom sill.
Acorns collected
from the Heath on well days.
Cat's cradle ropes
intertwine in the tree
filling the window
fingering the sill.
Seed and peanut feeders
hang like inverted
Christmas candles
for the small birds:
robins, tits, wrens.
When I leave she warns:
Don't forget to feed the squirrels
with a wildness of her own
and fills my pockets
with acorns as I stare
at the bare window
curtained in eucalyptus.

One Memory

His youngest grandchild
high as his knee, stood
before him inside the front gate.

Inclining his head he spoke slowly
looking seriously into her eyes,
hands searching for sweeties

in his jacket pocket.
The giant bow on top
of her head flopped back

made her feel again
for a second, not a person
but the Doll her father called her.

She gazed up, eyes larger
than the Mint Imperials granny
doled out of a tin years later.

She doesn't remember his words or sweets
only his smile and the kindness
that disppeared alongside him.

Aged Four

Sam's a tiny Northern
Lights, a flutter of small
birds buoyant as blown leaves
on winter grass. I play
the clavichord
after lunch. He stands
watching my fingers and face,
knows where feeling
is, and watches,
under the open lid,
as tangents strike.
A Christmas child
lit with sound and silences.

Politics

Centuries after the burning
we wait under dead-streetlamps
in the threat of rain
for fireworks on the Pont Corneille
to celebrate Jeanne d'Arc.

By the rail on the quai
a blond local, a young father
with patience like suspended time
takes off, ear by ear, the spectacles
of his sleepy son, and pockets them.

The child half sits on the square pillar,
half lies in his mother's arms
as she quietly croons to him
before the sky blazes over.

The husband's gaze circles,
tenderly, both woman and child.
I feel I cannot not stare
at this crop-haired angel in a cheap suit,
his left hand lightly resting
on his wife's rain-coated buttock.

While fireworks pirouette and flame
enveloped in distorted music
I wonder what he watches.
His wife continues to ignore him.
A big boned, street-wise woman
soft with her son,
and fidgety with her feet.

Naming the Herbs

This is the house of the apple.
Beneath it and the cellar
are fifteen acres of apples.
There are no streets here,
no lovers, no dogs,
neither the old nor the young.

On the ground floor
I sit in an empty room
on a straight-backed chair
tapping with impatient fingers
the knife, the fork,
the cup on my knee.
The westerly sun spills into the room
splashing its way among the surfaces,
nothing impedes the strangeness
that rustles across the floor.

A woman stands
laughing in the doorway
throwing bouquets of herbs
across the polished floor.
Hyssop. Rosemary. Rue.
A thousand names
to remember and forget.
This house is my apple,
time become green.

Shall I find the tree?
the carving of the cardinal points?
the mysterious stone?
I have searched
and found too much
to unravel or to comb
so I sit here bare-legged
in a bare room
greening my fingers.

The Moon's Song

I am the mother of pearl moon
mirror, incandescence, a thousand burnishing centres
smoothing scattered horses over the willow plain.
I am the deciduous dusk succulent as a gioconda
ocean's ebb and flow altering passion and place
powder drops on a near, dear-blue sea.
Foam speckled water feeds like a lover
the dolphin, the seahorse and the cuttle.

At dawn the owl prowls in the wood
sleep blossoming on his eyelids like illumination
the edges of the forest glisten.
All is up now and clear, day is an emerald forgetting.
Dark returns, descends among salt marsh seas
petals of star scatter seeds to open the heart.
I have a husband, a husband who is feathered and white
and oh, he sings to me, sings to me in the fern dark wood.